INTRODUCTION TO UNDERSTANDING PSYCHOPATHOLOGY:

A Psychoanalytic Perspective

INTRODUCTION TO UNDERSTANDING PSYCHOPATHOLOGY:

A Psychoanalytic Perspective

Ivan Sherick, Ph.D.

IPBOOKS.net
International Psychoanalytic Books

International Psychoanalytic Books (IPBooks),
Queens, NY
Online at: www.IPBooks.net

Interior book design by Maureen Cutajar, gopublished.com

ISBN: 978-1-949093-25-4

Preface

Formerly, I've written books on development throughout the life cycle, *Introduction to Child, Adolescent, and Adult Development: A Psycho-analytic perspective for students and Professionals*, and on clinical technique with people of all ages *Psychoanalytic Technique with Children, Adolescents, and Adults: An introduction for Students and Professionals*. Both of these books were written as introductions to the respective topics from a psychoanalytic perspective, with students and beginning professionals in mind as potential readers. Neither was a scholarly written book with references embedded in the text, nor with footnotes. A list of references was included at the end of these books, so that interested readers could immerse themselves more thoroughly in the topics. Technical terms were defined and the tone of these books was intended to be welcoming and not intimidating. The following book on psychopathology is written with the same goals as the above-mentioned books.

This book on the topic of psychopathology from a psychoanalytic perspective is not meant to be an all-encompassing exposition on the topic. Rather, it is meant to be an introduction. My psychoanalytic orientation is a contemporary ego psychology. Thus, it is classical but has integrated contemporary revisions that advance our thinking.

Please keep in mind that the term "psychopathology" is not meant by me to connote something ominous, malignant, or life threatening such as cancer or coronary problems. That is **NOT** what I am speaking about. The inclusion of the term "pathology" unfortunately may mean something biological and diseased to you. As a psychoanalyst my interest is in the **mind** and in **feelings, not the brain**. For example, when I talk about a depressed feeling I am **not** thinking of a biologically caused depression but one that is **reactive to a disappointment.** What is disappointing to one person is trivial to another. It is very subjective and based on one's life experiences and one's wishes, either attainable or fantastic. What I am mainly going to write about are the kinds of mental conflicts that evoke feelings and possible psychological disturbances that are common among almost all people. In fact, psychoanalysts often refer to non-patients including themselves as "normally neurotic."

On the other hand, I do not mean to minimize the degree of discomfort that mental conflict can cause many people. Obviously, it can be intense enough that an individual will seek professional help, or regretfully, contemplate suicide.

I will not be discussing the Autism spectrum, Asperger syndrome, or Psychosis. I have no experience with patients dealing with these diagnostic issues. The first two are very likely due to some kind of organicity and do not get referred to psychoanalysts. There are some analysts who have specialized in working with psychotic patients, but I am not one of them.

Occasionally, I will address a particular issue more than once insofar as it is important throughout the life cycle. Sometimes in the narrative I use the accepted contemporary convention when the gender of a subject is unknown, e.g., "parent", the pronoun "they" and the possessive "their", instead of "he or "she" and "his" or "her".

Table of Contents

Preface v

1. Essential Concepts in Understanding Psychopathology 1

2. Life Events and Psychopathology 11

3. Basic Biological Functions That May Be Drawn into
   Mental Conflict 21

4. Natural Strengths Interfered with by Mental Conflict 27

5. Diagnostic Categories 29

6. Childhood Psychopathology. 35

7. Adolescent Psychopathology 45

8. Adult Psychopathology. 51

   Postscript. 63

   Representative List of Topics 65

   Recommended Readings 67

CHAPTER 1

Essential Concepts in Understanding Psychopathology

There are some essential concepts needed in our efforts to understand psychopathology. These concepts are relevant in manifestations of psychopathology across the life cycle. We believe that a major, if not the most significant, motivator of the human psyche to be *instinctual drives*. We focus on two drives, namely, *libido* or the *sexual* drive, and *aggression*.

Both of these go through a linear sequence that we call, oral, anal, phallic, and Oedipal. In the early phases of drive development, sexual and aggressive drives are intermingled. It is only during the later phases that they autonomously distinguish themselves

Our clinical observations suggest that drives also have passive and active aims. The active aim is to achieve gratification via the expression of a drive wish towards an object and the passive aim is to have it expressed by an object towards oneself. The term "object" is used to differentiate a person from oneself, the "subject."

Examples of the active expression of the sexual and aggressive drives of the different phases follow. Keep in mind the passive expression would be where the subject obtains gratification by being the recipient of the expression of the drive by another person. An oral expression of the sexual drive is to suck, of the aggressive to bite or cannibalize. An example of the anal sexual drive is to pleasurably defecate, of the aggressive drive to mess or damage via a bowel movement. *Sadism* and *masochism* also arise in force during this phase. An example of a phallic sexual drive is to penetrate another body, of the aggressive drive to forcibly violate another body. Children express phallic aggressiveness, boys particularly, as if the body is a missile that can rapidly move though the space they occupy. *Exhibition* and *voyeurism* are also prominent sexual and aggressive drive expressions during the phallic phase. Around the same time as the phallic phase, the biological act of urination holds the attention of children. Boys will hold their penis as if it is a water hose and girls will try to stand up like boys while urinating. Before puberty, urination can be a discharge of libidinal excitement. Urethral aggression is to "piss" on something or somebody. Both genders are aware of their genitalia and frequently touch that area because it is pleasurable. It is no longer accepted theory that all girls are envious of a boy's penis because it is visible. Girls soon discover the part of their genitalia that is most pleasurable is in the interior.

Derivatives of the phases of drive are expressed in later stages of life development. I'm thinking of latency, the stage after the dissolution of the Oedipal stage and before the advent of puberty, the various stages of adolescence, the young adult years, and stages of adulthood into old age. It is more complicated than this, e.g., there are non-linear occasions, but for our purposes it will suffice to think of drive development as linear.

Drives have biological origin and seek pleasurable gratification. Gratification is a demand, not necessarily a conscious one, of the drive made upon the subject experiencing the drive. Life experience will either allow for pleasurable gratification or denial of such causing an experience of frustration, sometimes in excessive amounts.

Individuals differ in the relative constitutional or in-born strengths of the drives. A fixation occurs when during a particular phase of drive development, there is either excessive frustration or gratification of the drive. For example, if a child is born with a relatively weak need to suck and ingest milk and later foods, during the oral phase, then excessive frustration will not result in a fixation at the oral phase. On the other hand, if there is a strong oral drive then even limited frustration will result in a fixation. We call this reverse balance between strength of an inborn drive and experiences of gratification and frustration the *complemental series.*

Fixation is a concept that seems to be rarely referred to in contemporary case presentations and articles examining psychopathology. Perhaps this is because of a de-emphasis on the role of drives in contemporary thinking. I think this is a mistake.

Fixation can be thought of as a sensitivity, a vulnerability, or a pre-readiness to assert a combination of drive expressions when a contemporary experience revives memories (not necessarily conscious) of the past experiences involved in the causation of the fixation.

Regression is another essential concept in understanding psychopathology. In our understanding, it refers to the tendency to re-experience, not necessarily consciously, a past experience set off by a *psychic* similarity between a contemporary experience and a past one. It is a fixation that is like a magnet that draws the current experience back to the past (regression), so that the former is given psychic meaning, or nuanced, by the past experience. For example, if an adult is micro-managed by another adult and told how to discharge or take care of a responsibility, it could be that this interaction reminds, again not necessarily consciously, the managed adult of being told often as a youngster by their mother that they had to use the toilet even though they did not feel the need to evacuate their bowels. So, a boss is reminiscent of their mother. The response of the managed adult, depending on their past history, could be to stall or to obey immediately. Some of the expressions could be not in the best interests of the adult. For example, the employee might say, "Do it your self!" or do the task in a sloppy way. Such expressions probably will cause stress or anxiety, and could lead to psychopathology. Of course, there are many possible derivative drive expressions depending on the personal history of the managed adult.

Young children when ill or when very tired and sleepy have been observed to temporarily regress to earlier phases and manifest behavior reminiscent of an earlier time in their lives, much to the distress of some parents.

There are no children without adults, in most instances, parents. Much of the structures of a person's personality dealing with life experiences are laid down in childhood. It is the parents and other adults, such as grandparents, relatives, siblings, teachers, etc., that are important influences in a child's life.

Setting limits is an essential parental responsibility. Some parents are hesitant to do so because they wrongly equate it with expressing anger towards a child. If children have the feeling that they can act on whatever they want to then they get scared because if they can, the belief is that they can damage the adults that care for them. Also, setting limits helps a child internalize regulatory structures that helps them be in control of instinctual drives.

The foundations of later adolescent and adult psychopathology are laid down in early childhood. Adolescents also struggle with age specific puberty. Adults too, of course, have age specific issues that they deal with. However, we know when we treat adults we are treating the child and/or adolescent "within" the adult. A successful psychoanalysis of an adult is one where the adult has helped the "child or adolescent self" within to grow up. The adult has used their mature Ego resources to reassure the internal child and/or adolescent that the anxieties they dread can be withstood and that mental conflicts can have more adaptive outcomes than the ones earlier accepted. Hopefully, too, the "joys" of one's earlier age can also be re-experienced.

We know that a parent's own experience of being parented will influence or shape the parenting of his or her own children. Also, their own individual style of parenting may exacerbate things. It is inevitable, that a parent's psychopathology will enter parenting of their children and deleteriously effect their child's development. We call this the *intergenerational transmission of psychopathology.* This is an essential concept in understanding psychopathology.

Mental conflict occurs when an individual feels, either consciously or unconsciously, that he or she is in danger if expression is given either in action or thought to a wish that seeks gratification. This judgment is made by the part of the mind we call the *Ego*. Wishes are expressions of drives or instincts that originate in the part of the mind that we call the *Id*. The danger can be "understood" to be the *loss of an object* (usually mother or later representations of the maternal figure), *loss of love, injury to their body* (castration), or *loss of approval by their conscience*. The danger of loss of the maternal object is known as *separation anxiety*, something children commonly experience. Mothers serve as auxiliary egos for young children, so the absence of the mother scares a child that demands of the external and internal worlds will not be met. The sense of danger is felt as *anxiety* or, *shame* or *guilt*. We call the conscience the *Superego*, and its disapproval is felt as guilt.

Anxiety is a unique feeling that humans feel when they imagine the dangers mentioned above. There often are physical accompaniments such as an increased heartbeat and perspiration. The Ego uses it defensive resources to modify or "erase" (repress) the thought or wish provoking the anxiety. If the defensive maneuvers are not successful, the anxiety will not be sufficiently diminished in intensity and it can reach a heightened state that we call *panic*. A panic attack is very unpleasant and scary to the victim.

Children differ as to their *anxiety tolerance*. Presumably this has some connection to the strength of their Ego. With such tolerance, panic is less likely to occur unless the anxiety becomes very intense. Also, the "calling into play" of ego defenses will be delayed. If the child has supportive adults and can use his or her words then an emotional "crisis" for the child may be avoided and psychopathology averted.

Additionally, if a child has a high degree of *frustration tolerance,* the urgency to find gratification for the drive can be extended until a more acceptable expression can be found. A "melt down" can be avoided and negative consequences for the child's sense of well being can be prevented.

The part of the mind that resolves conflict we label as the *Ego*. Essentially it is the part of the mind that is in charge of executive processes like judgment. The wish that may be objectionable is then either modified or "locked away." *Symptoms* occur when the wish is modified sufficiently so its expression provides some modicum of gratification along with some degree of felt sanction demanded by the individual's internalized moral system (Superego) or by the rules and perceived demands of the external world. Essentially, symptoms are *compromise formations*. Early on, in childhood, the parents are the principle conveyers of the moral principles of the community. These are later internalized (the child's "inner policeman"), for the most part, by five or six years of age, with some modifications as the person ages.

Anna Freud proposed difference among conflicts based on their genesis, *intrapsychic, internalized*, and *external*. These three types of mental conflict are present throughout the life cycle. Intrapsychic is based on the inherent conflict between some wishes. Sometimes a person wants to be **active** in expressing a drive towards another being and sometimes they want to be the **passive** recipient of the expression of their wish. For example, an active wish to hit another person can be in conflict with a wish to be hit by the same person. Bisexual wishes can be in conflict, so that a subject may seek someone of the same gender or opposite gender to gratify a sexual urge. Ambivalence, loving and hating the same person, is another example of an intrapsychic conflict.

In an internalized conflict the structures of the mind are in conflict, i.e, the Ego feels anxiety or guilt (Superego) because a wish demands to be gratified but the Ego judges that if they execute the unmodified wish in action the Self will be punished.

External conflict is between the Ego and the external world, when the Ego judges that external rules are opposed to the expression of a wish in action. The wish must be modified to be acceptable.

Conflict cannot be completely avoided but the Ego has resources to minimize conflict in the first place so that psychopathology is not very intense and of shorter duration. This asset is called *ego strength*.

Children demonstrate individual differences in this asset. Intelligence is a favorable asset but the child has to be able to use it in beneficial ways that are more likely to exist based on good parenting and socialization. A good preschool education can help the child learn how to deal with peers in a mutually satisfying manner. Ego strength is demonstrated by resilience in the face of a stressful situation that may briefly render a child anxious and scared. A child possessing ego strength has a capacity to communicate so that adults can come to his aid. Feelings can be regulated often by the use of words rather than actions that can make stressful situations worse.

As the child ages, psychological processes develop that are able to modify objectionable drives. The outward expressions become more acceptable to other children or adults, thereby reducing external conflict. These processes are called ego defenses, and a child having ego strength has a repertoire of them. Also, he or she is cognizant of internalized moral edicts so that guilt is minimized. Ego strength will be an asset for the emerging adolescent and later for the young adult, as well as during adulthood. With reasonable limits a child might object but internally the child will feel safer and anxiety avoided.

As children age a process called *sublimation,* an aspect of ego strength, becomes a possibility. Herein, a drive wish, either sexual or aggressive, can be modified by a consolidated stronger Ego, so that the wish is expressed in a more socially acceptable form. A former unmodified aim to injure an animal may have caused feelings of guilt. Now a sense of beneficence can replace the guilt because of the expression of a more socially acceptable aim. An example could be a child that once harbored sadistic wishes towards a sib's pet, wanting to injure and kill the pet, in high school volunteers at a university laboratory doing experiments on animals to test out antibiotics. This same child that once wanted to harm pets later as an adult becomes a veterinarian.

Psychological mindedness is a trait we usually do not apply to a child, but to adolescents and adults. It is possible, however, that a precocious child may have such a trait. Having such a trait can allow someone to have insight that the unease they are feeling may be caused by some mental conflict. Consequently, they may be better able to resolve it and avoid greater distress.

Sadism and masochism are component sexual and aggressive drives arising in prominence during the anal stage. Derivatives of these two drive components continue throughout the life cycle. As mentioned above, the possibility of sublimation may play a role averting issues of unconscious feelings of inferiority, shame, and guilt that these two drives can generate for people.

Consciously, sadism involves the absence of guilt in dominating and controlling others. The sadist has a sense of being ordained with an omnipotent destiny. Masochism predominantly takes two forms, sexual masochism and moral masochism. In the former an adolescent or adult person may engage in fantasies or behavior wherein he or she is sexually humiliated and experiences pain, and subsequent orgasmic pleasure. In the latter, moral masochism, the individual seeks to suffer. This involves the relationship between the Superego and the Ego. During internalization of the parental objects in the structuralization of the Superego, de-sexualization, more-or-less, of the parental objects, occurs. In moral masochism a re-sexualization occurs. The child behaves in ways to be punished. Guilt is not experienced in most case. Depressive feelings later may accompany moral masochism. In some instances self-imposed unpleasure experienced by the moral masochist may be an unconscious way to try to win parental love, if the child believes they may be punished or that love will be withdrawn.

Trauma is another essential concept in understanding psychopathology. When an individual is unprepared to experience excessively intense incoming stimulation, they are overwhelmed. I mean that their psychic apparatus, parts of their mind, is overwhelmed or unable to process the incoming experience. This is what we mean by trauma. The effects of trauma, memories laid down in the mind, are that when the memory (memories) is re-stimulated or re-experienced by contemporary events, a feeling of being overwhelmed is re-experienced.

We think of two different kinds of trauma, *shock trauma* and *cumulative trauma.* The former refers to a single intense overwhelming experience. Examples might be, a car accident, witnessing the murder of a parent, experiencing rape, physical assault, etc. Cumulative trauma might be the result of a verbally abusive parent, experiencing racial derisive comments over the years, poverty, etc.

The effects of trauma can be delayed or manifested immediately. Some childhood traumas are experienced not until adolescence when a sexual encounter may re-stimulate memories of sexual abuse in earlier childhood. Adults who have witnessed or experienced massive terror experiences such as armed combat may return to civilian life with a post-traumatic syndrome (PTSD). For these individuals the past and present are intermingled so that a loud noise may trigger a fear reaction reminiscent from a past feeling of being near an explosion from a bomb or artillery fire. Such traumatized individuals experience a panoply of feelings like shame and anger. To get some distance from these unpleasant feelings dissociation and solitariness may follow. Difficulties sleeping and nightmares may be an affliction.

Some events for children that are planned even with supportive preparation may nevertheless prove to be traumatic. If the unexpected "negative" event has a particular meaning for a specific phase of development the interference can be experienced as a traumatic external conflict. For example, a tonsillectomy or appendectomy happening during the phallic phase when surgery is experienced as an assault on the body, can heighten castration anxiety. Psychosexual development can come to a halt and entry into the Oedipal stage might be stalled.

Narcissism is the wellbeing that is felt when a libidinal investment is directed at the self. Very early in life before there is much differentiation between the newborn and others we theorize that all libidinal investment is on the beginning self. We know better, now, that the infant seems invested in the maternal caregiver very soon after birth. Soon the growing infant receives loving expressions from the other people in his or her life. This is felt as secondary narcissism.

Acceptance later from an internalized Superego is felt as love, too. Later we will discuss psychopathology resulting from an over-inflated narcissism (narcissistic personality) and deflated narcissism (e.g., a constituent of dependency, depression, and other "bad" feelings.)

Self-esteem is a derivative of narcissism. It is the positive sense that comes from a feeling that one is a valued person, and others share this belief. Many children feeling peers do not choose to play with them on the playground, adolescents who feel unpopular or those whose girlfriend or boyfriend have ended with them, adults that are not invited to social events, etc., feel diminished self-esteem. We all seek to feel some degree of social acceptance insofar as we are social beings. However, if we are too dependent on such we are at risk to become depressed. One needs to feel good that they have achieved an accomplishment **even if** others do not applaud you. Here one's reservoir of healthy self-esteem is a safeguard. Otherwise you may be vulnerable to be hurt by the competition and envy of peers and colleagues.

CHAPTER 2

Life Events and

Psychopathology

The death of a loved one almost is always experienced as a terrible loss. Grief and stress are felt. It can be a family member's death, a friend or even a beloved pet. When you love a person your self-identity includes that person. The expectation, even though, you know better, is that they will be in your life forever. For parents it is unimaginable that a child will die before you do. We now appreciate the terrible loss that is felt by parents of an infant miscarried during a pregnancy or of a stillborn infant. There is a tendency on the part of young parents to want to get pregnant again to have another child. The newborn child is a "replacement" for the one who died. To be such is a psychological burden for the replacement child. He or she psychologically "carries" the bereaved parents' expectations for the dead child. For the parents and themselves they are not a "person in their own right."

For a child, particularly, the loss of a pet is very tragic. Pets offer companionship. Like adults experiencing the death of an offspring, a child may opt for another pet to replace the one that died. After the death of a loved one or pet a process of *mourning* takes place. This is a time of remembering the lost person or pet by privately having memories of them. This is a healthy process that enables the surviving individual to "let go" of the dead person or pet. It is an emotional acceptance that they are 'gone" and that "life goes on" for oneself without them.

Regretfully, some people are unable to satisfactorily mourn and instead they become depressed. This depression can last a long time and for some it becomes part of their *self-identity*.

Some individuals need to deny the personal loss. It may be they fear grieving because they imagine that if they allow that feeling, it will be overwhelming. For others, dependency on the dead person or pet is intense and imagining a lack of gratification is unbearable.

Young children were once thought to be unable to mourn but we know better now. A supportive adult can provide the child satisfaction of his or her basic needs, and with that support a child will feel the grief of the loss of the loved one. Distress leading to psychopathology may be avoided. Parental illness can also frighten a child. The loss of a loving, comforting, need-satisfying parent can terrify a young child. An adult that "steps-in" can help such a child.

Suicide of a family member, a parent or a sib, is a trauma that "doesn't go away." Especially devastating to a parent is the suicide of a child. Often the child was an adolescent when he or she suicides. The ubiquitous expectation of parents is that our children will survive us. The survivors will think of reactions that they wish they had done differently. For example, why didn't they get the guns out of the house, why didn't they seek out an in-patient treatment facility when their child expressed suicidal intentions, etc? Often, the parents will be overcome with grief. It is very difficult to see the children of their friends growing up and progressing through life. For the child survivors of a parental suicide, self-blame is often a guilty feeling. The adult child may feel they should have been more involved with a depressed parent. The guilt generates depressive feelings. For many, they are puzzled why they were not "enough" for the parent to stay alive. Anger may follow directed at the dead parent, followed by guilt.

Many adolescents, and adults too, may have suicidal thoughts but will not act upon them. These may occur if they are feeling rejected by peers or after a relationship has ended not by their choice. Such thoughts are common although not ubiquitous.

There is a phenomenon known as *survivor guilt*. An example might be if a group of adolescents are in an auto accident and there is as fatality. A survivor may feel guilty, especially if he or she was the driver. The superego of the survivor presumably must hold a memory of some transgression in the survivor's mind and uses this to make the individual feel guilty. Such an individual may get in some kind of trouble in order to be punished.

Another traumatic experience is to grow up in a family of survivors of genocide, e.g., the Holocaust. The surviving parents do not talk about their experiences but it casts a shadow over the family. The children sense the depressive feelings of their parents. Pathological identification with the parents in different forms can occur. The surviving child, for example, may grow up with a foreboding feeling of a terrible event "lurking around the corner."

Adoption has the best of intentions but regretfully it brings with it psychological consequences for all involved. What better intentions than to provide a family for a child given up by a birth mother for a number of reasons. Also, there are the benevolent aims of a family, perhaps unable to conceive a child of their own, to allow for parental gratification in caring for a child given up for adoption.

One should keep in mind, that what follows is not meant to be applicable to all instances of adoption. There are many instances of "good" outcomes in adoption. However, starting with the birth mother, who may have conceived the child out of wedlock while a teenager, there will be eventual guilt in having given up her infant, possibly unconscious. Of course, now we have so-called "open-adoptions," where the birth mother (parents) is involved in the life of the child. I doubt, however, if this is sufficient to mitigate the guilt generated by the knowledge of having given up her child for adoption.

I have been critical of "open adoptions" insofar as I believe that a young child can only be confused by having "more" than one mother. Also, the task of early childhood is to feel emotionally connected and integrated into a family. Having "another family" can only make this task more difficult and even impossible. The adoptive parents often harbor guilt, albeit unconscious, about having "taken away" the child from the birth mother. Also the fact of adoption is often not sufficient for adoptive parents to reduce feelings of inferiority having to do with "barrenness." Infertility can be an assault on one's masculinity or femininity.

There is much variability among adoptive parents as to when and if they tell their child he or she is adopted. Most disclose it insofar as it is difficult to keep it a secret. Many speak to the infant as being "special" and "chosen" from the beginning. Of course, for an infant this has no meaning, although the positive feeling emanating from the parent likely is experienced by the infant. Others may wait to tell the child until they are older. To me it makes most sense to wait, if possible, until the mid-latency years when the child will have the intellectual abilities to understand what "adoption" means. During the earlier years it is beneficial for the child to engage in the Oedipal struggle and telling the child about being adopted is likely to interfere with this engagement.

Sometimes an adoption occurs in a family that already has biological children, but because of social, ethical, and moral beliefs, adoption takes place to provide a family for a disadvantaged baby. The biological child, in such a family, may understand and endorse his or her parents' beliefs, but, nevertheless, unconsciously, they may wonder, "Was I not enough to satisfy my mother's (father's) parental needs?"

Then there is the adoptee. As the child grows there could develop a sense of abandonment by the birth mother (father). "Why was I given up for adoption?" A child is apt to blame him or herself for being inadequate in some way. Even an "open − adoption" may not reduce such feelings.

As the child enters adolescence, assuming they have been told of their adoptive status, an interest in searching for the birth parents may start. Sometimes, the occasion of reunion can be a satisfying one for both parties but sometimes it can be very disappointing. If the birth mother gave the child up for adoption, for whatever reason, but maintained parenting with other biological children, learning that can cause an adoptee a great deal of befuddlement as to why they were given up for adoption, but siblings were not. Again, there is a tendency to blame oneself.

As I review the consultations I have conducted over the years, divorce, has been an issue for many of the patients, seeking help. This is another social-psychological event that is involved in the genesis of psychopathology. Divorce, as a factor in causing distress, occurs across the lifespan. Thus, it affects not only the children, adolescents, and adults whose parents got divorced but also the adults engaged in a divorce.

Again, the children of all ages from a divorced marriage often blame themselves, consciously or unconsciously, that if they had been better behaved then their parents would have experienced less marital tension and would not have divorced. They believe this even though they often believe they could never please one or other parent. I suppose, sometimes there may be a modicum of truth to this belief. Parents can disagree as to the nature of parenting. Some believe in setting limits and some do not. This can cause spousal bickering and the children blame themselves. Children witnessing fighting between parents feel helpless. It becomes more difficult to control anger. Sometimes, one parent, in the eyes of the child, takes the role of the "bad cop" and the other the "good cop." This befuddles the child and makes them anxious.

There is often unconscious guilt for a child because of Oedipal wishes to divide the parents and to win the favor of the positive (opposite gender) Oedipal object. When this occurs in reality, the child, because of unconscious omnipotent beliefs feels responsible.

A child of divorce often will feel divided loyalties for each parent. Often this manifests itself in the child having feelings about visitation differences between the parents. Children often hold one parent responsible for the divorce. Loyalty tensions can be exacerbated if a parent begins to date and gets attached to another adult. If the child or adolescent "likes" this new person in their lives, the loyalty conflict can be exacerbated. For adolescents, knowledge that one of the parents is engaging in sexual encounters, they may feel that this parent is "cheating" on the other parent, even though they are divorced. Of course, if the parents are only "separated" and not divorced this feeling will be intensified. The adolescents' own sexual tension may be exacerbated in ways more intense than what normally occurs due to "primal scene" fantasies in an intact family. Primal scene fantasies refer to the ubiquitous fantasies of children that involve imagined sexual interactions of their parents.

For adults engaged in a separation or a divorce there are feelings of failure about his or her own ability to be intimate and committed. Also, guilt about causing the children emotional distress is ubiquitous.

Parents involved in a divorce are often emotionally distressed and unavailable to their children. After divorce a mother may have to seek employment and will be less available for her children. Often they themselves have been the children of a divorce. Their parents' divorce may have been a reaction to infidelity. Now as married adults, adultery may be a determinant causing marital strife and divorce for them. Once again, the intergenerational transmission of psychopathology is evident.

One could debate whether marital tensions should never end in divorce for the "sake" of the children in the family. The parents could avail themselves of marital therapy and be an example for their children of their attempts to resolve tension. However, there are instances where such intervention will not be helpful and one could argue it is better for the children to no longer witness daily fighting between their parents and to have the opportunity to experience happier parents in new relationships. Divorced spouses often feel intense anger towards their ex-spouses and most children sense this. This exacerbates already existing loyalty conflicts.

Alcoholism is another frequent behavior that can tear apart a marriage. Spouses and children suffer. When these children grow up, they too may be prone to alcoholism. Some of this may be an inherited predisposition to alcohol intolerance but some of it may be an identification with the parent.

Sexual abuse has far reaching consequences that often are determinants in the genesis of psychopathology. I am considering acts as abuse wherein the child is encouraged to participate in sexual acts with the adult. This may be the result of forcible participation, but it can also be based on exploiting the child's affection for the parent. Its victims in family settings are mostly young or adolescent girls and the perpetrators are fathers. Boys are not exempt from being victims of sexual abuse. Rarely this occurs in a family setting but most often in predominantly male dominated settings such as boarding schools for boys and involvement with Catholic clergy.

It is not sexual abuse when two preschoolers explore each other's genitalia. This is very common and does not involve exploitation but rather natural curiosity. If one of the participants was much older then I would consider it sexual abuse because of the power differential. In this instance the younger child likely will be frightened by the larger size of the older child's genitals.

I also consider it sexual abuse when there is extreme immodesty practiced by parents, so that their children witness their nudity a lot of the time. Also, some parents do not take measures to be private by closing doors or waiting till the children are asleep when engaging in sexual acts with their partners. Noises emanating from the parental bedroom can awaken children and scare them.

Adults, mostly females, are also subject to sexual abuse. In almost all cultures men have privileges such as expectations to be the more assertive gender when it comes to heterosexual encounters. Regretfully, this social/cultural assignment can be distorted in an exaggerated way. This can be especially in situations of a power discrepancy between a man and a woman, e.g., in a supervisor-supervisee situation or employer-employee situation. Unfortunately, there can be real or imagined consequences for refusal to comply. Another impossible situation is when the perpetrator is a family member. It is hard for a young girl to refuse the advances of an admired father, uncle, or older male cousin. Hence, sexual abuse or more commonly sexual harassment can be the result. Feminine activism is on the rise and women are more likely to publically make known their opposition to such male behaviors and publicize the identities of perpetrators. Also, women now have the expectation that sexual involvement be consensual. Adult women have had to overcome hurt, shame and feelings of responsibility to publically express they have been victims.

The effect of sexual abuse is individually variable, although never positive. For the child victim as they mature into adolescence or adulthood, sexual inhibition or promiscuity can be a consequence of the earlier experience of sexual abuse. A relationship with a supportive partner can help a victim who is sexually inhibited to overcome this symptom.

Physical abuse without sexual violation also can contribute to psychopathology. The victim will be terrified that a beating will occur again. Often with children, my experience is that an alcoholic father is often the perpetrator. Mothers that are alcoholic may also resort to physical abuse but this is less common.

Emotional abuse can also be experienced by people of all ages. A disturbed parent may do such to his or her child, constantly undermining the child's self-worth. It is as if the child's very essence, the "soul," has been damaged. A spouse or partner in a relationship can also be emotionally abusive. The victims often *dissociate* or "escape" from their self- identity. This kind of severe emotional abuse has been labeled "soul murder."

In my view, the advent of Internet pornography has contributed to male deviant sexual behavior. It is very accessible to even pre-teens who have smart phones and access to the Internet. In pornographic depictions of sexual encounters between men and women, there is no emotional relationship between the two participants. The sexual act is the predominant reason for the encounter. I believe this encourages the same in real encounters and it is not healthy for heterosexual relationships to not have an emotional connection and can lead to more problems. Of course, it is also a possible outcome in depictions of sexual encounters between same gendered participants.

Regretfully, when one is a victim of abuse of any kind, there may be a tendency to identify with the abuser. This is the Ego's way of trying to master a negative or traumatic experience endured passively by actively recreating it with someone else as the victim. Earlier, this was alluded to when we discussed the intergenerational transmission of psychopatholgy.

The birth of a sibling is usually an event that a child has little influence in causing. Sometimes an "only child" can tell its parents that they wish for a sibling to play with. This can be impactful for some parents. Many children look upon a newborn sib with curiosity. Some want to hold them. Some wish they would disappear. In cases where the latter feelings are evident, parents need to be watchful because the older child's hugging can be very intense and potentially suffocating of the newborn. If a sib were to die because of illness, the surviving sib that wished the death will likely fear retribution most of the remainder of his or her life.

It can be a narcissistic injury to an existing child when a sib is born. They may feel hurt and wonder why their parents needed another child. Were they not sufficient? Was he or she lacking in some way.

They feel competitive and envious of the aging sib's talents and skills. They may perceive that the sib has a better relationship with one of the parents than he or she does. This makes them feel loved less than the sib. This can be true insofar as the child's latent angry feelings, maybe unconscious, have interfered with expressions of affection for the parent. The parent may feel this as rejection and seek closeness with another child.

These feelings of sibling rivalry can last forever. The child now an adolescent may compare themselves to the sib in a number of areas. For example, who is the better athlete, more achieving in school, accepted to a better university, has a more beautiful girlfriend or handsome boyfriend, etc?

As an adult the envy can be about the attaining of a graduate degree, the income earned on the first position upon graduation, etc. These competitive, jealous, and envious feelings all can make the adolescent or adult feeling such, either consciously or unconsciously, insecure, feeling like a failure, unloved and depressed. In some instances where a sibling has a handicap, another sib might look more inept than he or she is, because they feel the need to underplay their own accomplishments so the disadvantaged sib will feel less badly.

Many times, a parent can feel towards their own child the same rivalrous feelings they felt towards a sibling. This is an example of *psychic reality* trumping *objective reality*. If this is so they may be less loving towards the child or, defensively, loving in an exaggerated way to cover over the hateful feelings for the child and from themselves. The child who is the recipient of such hateful feelings originating from the parent's past relationship with his or her own sib, will feel unloved. If this dynamic happens early during infancy, a reactive attachment disorder could be the result.

Being a victim of racial bigotry is being a victim of sadism. I include this in this section on life events and psychopathology because the color of one's skin is not elective. People who are members of racial minorities come up against sadistic slurs frequently. It causes the victim to feel isolated, alien, and reactively angry. Having a support group is of immense benefit. Belonging to a minority religion can also evoke bigots to deliver insults and in some instances physical attacks. I am thinking of anti-Semitism and anti-Muslim feelings. Members of these groups who are observant may worry about being attacked and may make efforts in public not to wear traditional garb so as not to be noticed. Doing so they may feel badly for having compromised their beliefs.

Basic Biological Functions That May

Be Drawn into Mental Conflict

Basic functions such as sleeping, eating, toileting, locomotion, and sex can all be drawn into early mental conflict, initially external but evolving into internalized conflict as the function is drawn into intrapsychic conflict. In some instances there may be a medical cause for the problem and it is wise to first rule out such with a pediatric consultation. Once there is confidence that a medical issue is not involved, seeking clarification for the cause of the problem via a psychological explanation makes sense.

Sleeping gets drawn into conflict often because of the management by parents of sleeping arrangement of infants. Some parents espouse having the newborn, and even older child, sleep in the same bed as the parents. It feels natural and convenient if the baby awakens in the night. This arrangement can present the youngster to be witness to parental intimacy. Overstimulation from parental noises and/or visual images disrupts the sleep of the infant or youngster. The input of noise and images do not make sense to a young child. It is best to have a child sleep in a different room.

Children during the phallic and Oedipal phases have fantasies of sexual intimacy that their parents are involved in. We call these fantasies "primal scene." They erroneously interpret the noises they hear as one parent hurting the other. This is particularly during the anal sadistic phase of psychosexual development. The result can be fear and worry that a parent whom they are dependent upon is being hurt. The result could be nighttime fear and disturbance of sleep.

A few children have "pavor nocturnus" where they walk in their sleep, having no conscious memory later of its occurrence. Potentially they could injure themselves. The cause of pavor nocturnus is unclear.

As the child ages, sleep disturbances can occur because of fearful fantasies of dangerous intruders, entering their bedroom in the middle of the night. The "intruders" are creations of the child's mind that are attributed to the external world, what we call *externalizations*. Sometimes they are monsters, sometimes humans. The fearful child resists falling deeply asleep to avoid being a victim. As the child gets older, rational thinking can offer some reassurance but derivatives retreat to the Unconscious and they can persist. Disturbed sleeping can be a feature of this person. Sleep can be disrupted, too, by *nightmares.*

Ordinarily the sleeping mind is able to process wishes that are forbidden to the awake mind. These wishes, images, and thoughts are disguised sufficiently so that the dreamer can express such forbidden contents in the form of a dream. Via such *dream work* some gratification is experienced in safety. However, when the disguise is insufficient it is like an alarm going off and the sleeping dreamer is awakened by a "nightmare." This dynamic can operate throughout the life cycle.

Eating is another basic biological function that can be involved in psychic conflict. What is very common is the phenomenon of "comfort eating." This is when eating food is not because of nutritional hunger but because of "emotional hunger." That is, ingesting food is an attempt, albeit often unconsciously, to "fill up" because of an internal sense of "emptiness." It is not that the stomach is empty but rather the sense of self-worth is depleted.

The feeling of fullness after eating is meant to conceal the inner emptiness. This could be resulting from a lack of relatedness to a cherished person, perhaps a maternal figure. The function of eating often is imbued with maternal meaning insofar as it is usually the mother who provides food for the infant and is watchful that they consume a sufficient amount of food. Hence, an individual will desire a scoop of ice cream but instead they will consume the whole quart. Putting on weight and resultant unhappiness is a casualty of this dynamic. In some rare instances after overeating a person may feel "orgiastic, but soon thereafter feel depressed."

Akin to the dynamic where food has more than nutritive value is a condition known as *bulimia*. An individual will overeat likely for similar reasons discussed in comfort eating, but then the individual forces vomiting as a way of getting rid of the increased calories they have eaten. Another eating disorder is known as *anorexia*. Here, an individual reduces considerably the amount of food they eat. Unconsciously they likely wish to consume a large amount of food, but defend against this by eating little. Such individuals will appear very thin, sometimes even looking emaciated. In our culture bulimia and anorexia predominantly effect adolescent girls and young adult women. This probably is because the female gender is assigned by both genders the task of appearing thin and shapely, not overweight.

Breast-feeding is a healthy relationship building interaction between mother and infant. It usually does not exceed a duration of one year, often sooner in our Western culture. In impoverished areas of the world a longer duration has major health protection benefits for the infant. Mothers often will wean their infants when teeth start to develop for the infant. Mothers do not welcome being bitten on the nipple. In instances where the weaning from the breast or bottle is much earlier that the infant desires, an oral sucking fixation can occur, especially if the constitutional drive to suck is strong. Such infants may become adamant later about thumb sucking. When mothers breast-feed for a very long duration, e.g., for periods of two years or more, I think they do it more to satisfy something they crave unconsciously, e.g., a stronger relationship with their own mother who was emotionally distant.

The function of toileting also can get drawn into conflict. As with the function of eating where food becomes an unconscious symbol of mother, in toileting the feces can unconsciously symbolize the mother. (I say mother and not father insofar as in our culture it is the maternal figure, not the paternal figure, that mostly is involved in toilet mastery.) The child undergoing toilet training (I prefer toilet "mastery") may defy the imposed restrictions and rules about where and when to defecate, especially if the constitutional strength of the anal drive is inherently strong. Here, the aggressive drive is being expressed along with the anal libidinal one. This child could be messy and even smear the feces, much in defiance of the mother. Or they may become constipated and controlling. The child that soils may unconsciously equate the scent of the beloved or depriving mother with the scent of feces. An extreme psychopathological expression of this soiling is called *encopresis* and this can last into latency until toilet mastery is complied with. For those children who resist defecating when told to do so, some parents may resort to giving the child an enema. This can be repeated many times. This is regrettable insofar as it causes the child to feel "invaded" and unsafe and can cause or strengthen an anal fixation.

Urinating and its control over-laps with the anal phase and the later phallic phase. Some children do not obtain bladder control and bed-wetting at night can be an issue. We call this *enuresis.* Assuming that there is not a medical cause, the issue can be a psychological one. Before a child is pubertal, sexual excitement cannot be relieved through ejaculation. Instead urination seems to be imbued with this function for some children, especially boys. A child who is inappropriately exposed to parental immodesty regarding nudity, or is involved in primal scene fantasies may be sexually excited, in some instances, and the outcome could be enuresis.

Something as basic as the biological function of locomotion can get caught up in conflict. Young children, who have had to wear braces to correct some physical ailment, may have difficulties with aggression when older. The clinical conjecture is that the inability to use their lower limbs and move about interfered with the discharge of aggressive energy. The aggression is "built up" and at a later age gets discharged.

Sexual expression often gets caught up in mental conflict for both genders. For men, issues of *early ejaculation* can deprive them and their partners with full pleasure. Also, *impotence* can result in a failure to get an erection and maintain it. This reduces self-esteem for the male. For some men, intromission is scary because unconsciously they view a vagina as capable of castrating them. Women may be unable to climax via sexual intercourse, requiring the use of a dildo to engage in excessive clitoral stimulation, or need to masturbate after coitus. This may demoralize both them and their partners. Both may feel inadequate. Again, ruling out a physical cause, psychological causation needs to be explored and mental conflicts resolved.

Some individuals may be afraid of sexual intimacy and avoid it. Instead masturbation provides relief. Many issues interfering with obtaining sexual discharge and pleasure seem to be related to unresolved Oedipal issues. For example, unconsciously one's partner may represent a parent and hence an illicit relationship to be avoided because of guilt and anxiety. These issues can remain throughout one's lifetime.

For many people, mostly young adults, bisexual conflicts may be involved in sexual tension. They may believe that being heterosexual is the cultural norm but may be aware of homosexual attractions. Afraid of being exposed and ostracized they inhibit all sexuality, sometimes even fantasy. In our contemporary society there is more acceptance of homosexuality for both genders but there still is either overt or subtle condemnation of the practice. A supporting group of like-minded friends can help an individual cope with such conflicts. Also, parents who support a child who is gay or a lesbian is very helpful in relieving shame. More about this later.

Gender issues are in the forefront of contemporary society. Many people object to the binary classification of gender, male or female. Some adolescents' feel very uncomfortable with the birth gender assigned based on anatomy. As adolescents they feel more akin with the gender opposite their own or with nei-ther. Some elect to have hormone treatment to hasten the development of the other gender's body; some elect also to have surgical interventions. Adolescents having *gender dysphoria* are very unhappy, even suicidal. A strong support group of like-minded adolescents and supportive parents is needed. More about this later.

CHAPTER 4

Natural Strengths Interfered
with by Mental Conflict

I turn my attention now not to basic biological functions but to inborn talents and inherent assets. Talents presumably have a biological foundation insofar as they manifest early in life and we see significant individual differences. For example, some toddlers seem to be very adept and precocious at crawling, walking, and climbing stairs. It is as if they have a muscular balance and strength that is inborn. Such toddlers differ from peers. Practice seems to transform the talent into a skill. When they grow up the child may demonstrate athleticism.

My conjecture is that "curiosity" is one such inborn talent. Being curious is an aspect of a mind that is creative. Individual differences exist. Alas, sometimes being curious can get caught up in mental conflict. If the curiosity is believed to be "too much" involved in sexual curiosity and/or *voyeurism,* then curiosity in general can be inhibited because of a moral condemnation by the child's Superego. If so, a learning disorder can ensue and the otherwise intelligent youngster can become an underachiever, and suffer all the unpleasant accompanying feelings connected to this label, e.g., shame.

There are other non-biological functions that can get caught up in mental conflict. I will mention a couple, so you have an idea of what I mean. If a child has the inborn talent and additional learned skills that allow for athletic participation but is conflicted about competition and exhibitionism, he or she may decide not to continue involvement in the sport. These conflicts may be unresolved from the Oedipal phase. The result is a loss of a potential enhancement of self-esteem for the individual.

Another inborn talent is musical ability. A person with such a talent can become a skilled virtuoso with a musical instrument or participate in chamber music or orchestral music. All of these activities can add to their pleasure and self-esteem. But not if they have excessive "stage fright." Two major contributors to this performance anxiety are conflicts with *exhibitionism* and *competition*. The former is an instinctual component of the libidinal phallic-Oedipal phase and the latter an aggressive derivative of the same phase. Intense stage fright may not allow such a performer to engage in performances or interfere with the quality of his or her performance.

CHAPTER 5

Diagnostic Categories

The diagnoses that I will employ essentially are *neuroses, psychoses*, and *character disorders*.

As a psychoanalyst my clinical efforts have been primarily made in clinical involvement with patients dealing with neurotic issues. My experience with psychotic individuals is absent. In part, such patients were not referred to me, or if in consultation I suspected psychotic issues were a major consideration, I referred the patient to a colleague.

There are patients that are diagnosed as *borderline*, referring to those whose issues seemed to be on the border between neurosis and psychosis. Such individuals might manifest psychotic symptoms in a temporary fashion but not in a sustained way. My experience with such patients has been minimal.

I will, however, mention the major features of this disorder insofar as it is often used as a diagnosis mainly with adults. There is a continuum of severity among borderline patients, as is the case for all diagnoses. Some borderline individuals will only occasionally, and then briefly, seem to go over the boundary into psychotic functioning. The two major defenses they employ are *splitting* and *projective identification*. In the former they divide people into good and bad with the former receiving loving feelings and the latter hateful feelings.

In projective identification borderline individuals attribute negative aspects of their own personality to another person. Then, the borderline person behaves towards that person in a manner that often tends to cause the person to respond with behavior originally attributed to them, thereby "validating" the borderline's critical perception of the person. Borderline individuals have difficulty particularly with regulating aggression and with reality testing.

In my years of clinical practice, my time has mostly been spent with patients dealing with neurotic issues, most to a degree that a neurotic diagnosis was warranted. As I said earlier, we all deal with mental conflict and the majority of people have been characterized as *normally neurotic*. Those who require professional attention have not been successful independently in overcoming or compensating for their maladaptive behaviors. Presumably, all could benefit from increased emotional understanding of the origin of their neurotic thinking and behaviors.

Depressive feelings seem to be universal when an individual is "disappointed" in life. They may have not attained a goal they were seeking, or a relationship that was promising was broken off, a job offer was not secured, etc. You can see that a disappointment underlies all of the perceived causes for the depressive feelings. The severity varies and is heightened by earlier life experiences that were felt to be due to "bad luck" or self-created. The severity can be reduced if supportive family, friends, colleagues, etc., comfort the depressed individual. Often depressive feelings prompt a person to seek professional therapeutic help. The depressed person need not be diagnosed as suffering from a primary depression that is incapacitating. When it is such, the person restricts his or her involvement with life effecting sleep, eating, relationships, work, etc. In modern day psychiatry this is characterized as an *endogenous* depression, thought to be biologically caused and treated primarily by anti-depression medication. Depressive episodes caused by non-biological causes are labeled as *exogenous.* Psychotherapy or psychoanalysis is the treatment of choice. For some individuals being depressed becomes a personality type or character style.

Neuroses occur when there is mental conflict between the Ego and the external world, or the internalized "rules" of morality lodged within the Superego.

Hence some drive expression is judged by the Ego as forbidden, anxiety and/or guilt is felt, and the drive/wish must not be expressed either in thought or action unless modified sufficiently, compromised to meet with perceived approval by the external world or Superego. Symptom formation, a compromise, can result and a neurotic diagnosis may be warranted.

Character, from a psychoanalytic perspective refers to a characteristic style or behavior that typifies a particular individual. It is like a "signature" of the individual. Hence, it is a ubiquitous feature of all people. It is like a "firewall" that an individual has habitually been perceived and acted in their world. When it is so exaggerated that it becomes a "feature" of the individual we give it a diagnosis, otherwise it is characterized with terms such as "he is full of himself (narcissistic)," or "he is so dramatic (hysteric)," or "he is so rigid (obsessional)," and so on.

Developmental Interferences occur when the external world, usually, parental figures, have unreasonable expectations, regarding their children. There are many such examples, some which will be addressed below, but I will give you a sense of what is meant. As mentioned above, a mother, to gratify her own needs, may prolong nursing at her breast, into her child's third year. Prolonged nursing can cause an oral fixation and a disturbed dependence on the mother. Another example, is expecting a youngster who does not yet have anal sphincter control to conform to toileting mastery. Failure is inevitable and a consequence can be unnecessary anger by both participants and an anal fixation.

Some developmental interferences are reversible while some are not. Some could lead to psychopathology at the time of occurrence while others have a delayed effect. We may not be able to decipher the reason for the delayed effect. In the future of the child an experience occurs that has a derivative meaning related to the original earlier interference, and a neurotic symptom may appear.

Developmental conflicts are unavoidable. Such conflicts are present throughout the life cycle. For example, during adolescence, girls and boys strive to be independent of their parents but they encounter resistance from parents who do not want to "let go." In adult years, developmental conflicts are mostly psychosocial, such as "the empty nest" syndrome, decisions to retire, etc.

I believe life's major developmental conflict to be the advent of the Oedipal Complex, usually occurring between three to six years of age. During the Oedipal phase children of both genders feel both sexual (loving) and competitive (hateful) feelings towards both parents. Usually predominantly positive feelings are felt towards the parent of the gender opposite to their own, and less intense positive feelings towards the parent of their own gender. Hostile, competitive feelings are felt in the opposite direction regarding intensity. The boy feels negative towards father and the girl the same towards mother. The boy wishes to impregnate his mother and the girl wishes to be impregnated by the father.

You can see that conflict is to be expected during this developmental stage. It is more or less resolved through suppression of the Oedipal complex, insofar as the boy fears hurtful physical retaliation from the father, comparable to his own active wish (*castration*) vis-à-vis his father, and the girl fears a loss of love from her competitor, mother, for father's exclusive attention. The partial dissolution of the Oedipal complex results in internalization of the imagined and/or real parental moral demands that confront the child, and the Superego structure is the outcome. A mental structure essentially is a complex of thoughts and feelings that endure over time, i.e., they have a "long expiration date." As mentioned earlier, the internalization of parental objects is a desexualized version of them.

An internalized Superego is a great benefit to a developing child insofar as it is sort of an "inner policeman" that assists the child in controlling drives. If the Superego is weak or corrupt because of parental deficiencies the Superego will later be a determinant of psychopathology. An example of this, is with pre-adolescents and older teenagers, where delinquency is a possibility. It is because of the benefits of an internalized moral system, and the negative consequences of its absence or inadequacies, that I deem the struggle with the Oedipal Complex to be of utmost importance in limiting or encouraging future mental disturbances.

The partial dissolution of the Oedipal Complex allows for the ushering in of Latency. During Latency the strength of the drives vis-à-vis the Ego is weakened and this is a time of learning about the "real world." It is no wonder that this phase corresponds with entry into school for many children. This includes recognition by the child that there are external rules and prohibitions they must observe. When puberty occurs the latent Oedipal feelings are re-strengthened and adolescents must struggle with them and come to a resolution of the conflicts that emerge. It is a time for latent psychopathology to become more obvious.

Adulthood ordinarily means leaving the security of the family and furthering the independence that began earnestly in adolescence. Some of the major events dealt with in becoming an adult can be fertile ground for mental conflict and potential psychopathology. This will be discussed further below.

Another category of diagnoses involves the body, or soma, and hence the category of *psychosomatic* disorders. The separation of the mind and the body is artificial. As psychoanalysts we focus on the mind, not the brain but we do not deny the existence of the brain. In contemporary science the intimate connection between the two is a future achievement. Also, the connection may turn out in some or many instances to be correlation and not causal. However, we do recognize there are some instances where a somatic illness seems to be triggered by psychic conflict. Often this is the case when a diagnosis is deemed to be functional or idiopathic, meaning a medical cause cannot be found. Presumably there are some instances when a physical illness triggers a mental disturbance. For example, receiving a diagnosis of cancer is likely going to result in tension, anxiety, and depressive feelings. It is possible an individual given that diagnosis may experience guilt and consider it to be punishment for some past transgression. Somatization often seems to affect the gastrointestinal system, although pain is another symptom cluster.

It may be that there is an underlying physical issue that could not be diagnosed and because of feeling as if he or she is being accused of malingering, psychic consequences like frustration and anger can result. An example in the past decade were patients, often women, who complained of chronic fatigue who were diagnosed as being functionally depressed. Although a definitive cause has not been confidently discovered, chronic fatigue is now believed to be a result of an infection or some metabolic issue.

Somatization should not be confused with *hypochodriasis*. Hypochondriacs worry excessively about coming down with physical ailments. Usually, this is infrequent among children and adolescents, and is more common among adults. You can see adolescents in cold weather wearing only a flimsy polo shirt while adults are wearing heavy overcoats. The adolescent is making a statement of independence from parents; they own their body and they will do otherwise than dictated by parents. Parents dress children warmly.

Hypochondriacs worry that every abdominal pain is a sign of a potential serious ailment, e.g., an ulcer, or a headache is a sign of a brain tumor, etc. Sometimes such people have identified with parents who also worried excessively about illness or were afflicted by one, sometimes fatal. A child or adolescent losing a loved parent may identify with the parent in an unconscious attempt to reunite with them. In some instances hypochodiasis may be unconscious anticipated punishment for some imagined or real transgression.

CHAPTER 6

Childhood Psychopathology

In this section I will discuss psychopathology that predominates in childhood. I believe that experiences of childhood are very significant in future psychopathology. In treatment I think psychoanalysts often talk of treating the child within the adult. Adult analysands are told either explicitly or implicitly that they have to assist their child self to grow up. However, I do not mean to convey that there is no plasticity in the mind. On the contrary, while continuity is very important discontinuous experiences can occur. For example, a child may have experienced parenting that was depriving, or even abusive, maybe absent, but later during their school years they come upon a very considerate and supportive teacher and some of the adverse effects of their earlier childhood are modified in a positive growth manner. Of course, the opposite is also true. An early positive growth experience with a considerate, caring, and developmentally sensitive parent will be reduced albeit not necessarily eliminated by the loss of the parent, for example through divorce or death. Childhood is a time when emerging strengths or dysfunction can develop.

Recall, too, what I said earlier about the *complemental series* so that individuals will be affected somewhat differently by the same experience based on inherited differences in the strength of their inborn needs. So what may be a negative experience for one child may be a negligible one for another child. The impact of an adverse experience will differ for various children based on the ego resources at their disposal.

Conflicts occurring early in life before the Oedipal phase of development are classified as *pre-Oedipal*. These conflicts are seen as external insofar as the structualization of the mind is only in its infancy so that conflict between the Id and the Ego, or the Id and the Superego are not yet an issue. The infant may have been sub-jected to weaning before it was ready, perhaps because of a strong constitutional strength of the oral sucking drive. Perhaps the mother may have experience a lack of milk because of her own biological reasons. Maybe, the infant was starting to bite the nipple and it hurt the mother so she weaned her infant.

Interactions between parents and children that are conflictual occurring during the anal and phallic stages are also considered preOedipal. Many of these external conflicts are avoidable inso-far as they result from parental demands that the child cease a behavior that is not pathological or which they are not advanced sufficiently in maturation to be able to comply with the external demand. For example, the infant with a strong drive to suck being weaned from the breast too early, or the toddler who does not yet have anal sphincter control maturation being asked to comply with toilet mastery, or the 3 year old who is harshly chastised for touching his penis and "masturbating." These are developmental conflicts that are due to misguided parenting; perhaps examples of intergenerationally transmitted pathological styles of parenting.

The consequences of such external conflicts are many and very variable based on individual differences in the persons involved. What I mean is the intensity of the frustration experienced by the child based on the strength of the thwarted instinctual expression, the degree of harshness of criticism evoked in the parent towards her or his child, whether or not physical punishment is meted out to-wards the non-complying child, etc. We will further explore the consequences of these *developmental interferences* and *develop-mental conflicts* later.

There are a whole group of infant behaviors attributed to errant early maternal relating by infants. The consequences are disturbed *attachment disorders* exhibited by the infant towards its mother or other caregivers. Reactive attachment disorders are behaviors that are peculiar to the presence of the maternal care-giving figure. The infant may show fearfulness, or perhaps disinterest, both behaviors that are contrary to the normal cheerful expressions of infants to the perceived presence of the maternal caregiver. Such infants are unable to form an emotional bond with her. Other infants may display a preference for stranger caregivers. As these infants get older, continued difficulties in the relationship to their maternal figures could be the harbinger of future psychopathology. Such children may engage in "baby talk," thereby revealing wishes to be taken care of by mother like a dependent baby.

In reviewing my notes of people who consulted with me over the years, many adults, and adolescents too, in our first meeting, convey a difficult relationship with their mothers and/or fathers. Of course, not being there, I cannot with great confidence say that some of these patients, as infants, would have had diagnoses of reactive attachment disorders. As adolescents or adults, they may display difficulties with becoming intimate with a partner, not empathic, and consequently loneliness can be an outcome for some. For others, they prefer to remain solitary. Adopted children often can exhibit difficulties in relationships with adults, often with adoptive parents. It is not surprising given that their life circumstances likely included adult neglect, sometimes in institutions, as well as fantasies of abandonment by birth parents.

Temper tantrums are a feature of some children. Their occurrence likely is due to a combination of factors, such as developmental immaturity of the brain in centers dealing with control of motor impulses, feelings, parental difficulties in setting limits, and insufficient internalization of the rule "use your words."

During a temper tantrum a child is out of control, thrashing about on the floor with his or her body, biting, throwing and breaking things, yelling and crying, etc. Upset parents have trouble restraining the child and it is best to make sure the child is safe, removing things that might hurt them, and let the temper tantrum run its course and end. In most instances, children "grow out" of temper tantrums by the time they enter Latency.

Procrastination can begin in childhood and become a habitual way of dealing with internal expectations of achieving goals. It is self destructive insofar as "waiting for the last minute" to begin to complete a task often only makes it harder to finish.

It can be a style of effort that can sabotage accomplishments in school and work. For some it begins with a sense that "no one is going to tell me what to do". A child growing up with a domineering and authoritarian parent could develop into a procrastinator. Such a person will be self-critical and vow to change but will put off doing so, only to intensify the shame they feel throughout life.

Learning disabilities affect children in primary school and can continue throughout their education. The difficulty can be limited or widespread. Only reading may be disrupted, *dyslexia*, or mathematical skills, or spelling, or writing, or the "whole gambit."

For most children who are very motivated to be like their peers, learning problems can cause a great deal of distress. Parental distress can exacerbate the problems. The cause(s) of learning difficulties are complicated and vary. Assuming no organic cause is a determinant, issues of achieving may be due to conflicts about competition, issues of diminished self- esteem based on a conviction that one is not "smart," issues of irrational gender inferiority, such as girls are not meant to master science and mathematics, etc.

Passive-aggressiveness is a defense utilized that can become a beginning character style and endure through adolescence into adulthood. Here aggressiveness is concealed in a manner that may go unnoticed by the recipient of its expression. For example, such a child reaching for the milk on the table may "accidentally" knock it over messing the table. The parent(s) may excuse it as clumsiness not recognizing it as an expression of hostility towards them. For the benefit of the child, hopefully, a parent will get suspicious that the child is expressing anger in a concealed way. Perhaps, then, the child can be encouraged to get in touch with the anger and use words to express it and the disturbed behavior can cease.

Another form of defensive behavior that can begin in childhood that can persist in later years is the use of the defense of *reaction formation*. Here too, as in passive-aggressive behavior, what is overt conceals what is felt latently or unconsciously. Affectionate behavior may be the opposite of what is more genuinely felt but forbidden, namely anger. Sometimes the opposite can be the dynamic, namely, forbidden love is expressed as anger. At some level, the child using reaction formation can feel duplicitous and guilt can be felt with little insight.

Childhood disturbances often present for the first time in a school situation. Much stress results for all the people involved with the child. Three such diagnoses are *conduct disorder, oppositional-defiant disorder*, and *attention deficiency-hyperactive disorder*. These issues can continue throughout the life cycle with different labels. The first two may be labeled delinquency or anti-social behavior in the adolescent or adult years.

A major feature of a child having a conduct issue is the impulsivity of the child. Rules of "waiting your turn," "using your words," "let someone else take a turn," do not seem to be accepted by the child. The child will be disruptive of the atmosphere of the intended calm classroom. Teachers with many children in the classroom will contact parents and with adolescents the student may be expelled.

A child presenting with an oppositional-defiant disorder, can create an even more stressful situation for all involved than a conduct disorder. This is because it is has a relational expression. The child is often "in the face" of the teacher, arguing and seeking to annoy the teacher. Presumably the child is displacing anger onto the teacher meant for someone else, perhaps a parent. The child may feel it is safer to express it outside the family.

Attention-deficit hyperactivity disorder creates havoc for the child. Learning is disrupted. In my experience this "disorder" is often a mistaken diagnosis, especially in a classroom with many children as in a public school. Many of these children are anxious and that is interfering with attention and contributing to what looks like hyperactivity. Defensive efforts against aggressive impulses secondarily interfere with concentration and learning. These children, in my opinion, need psychotherapy and not drugs to quell their behavior. The anxiety may be due to many different factors, such as those discussed above. Of course, there are children with an ADHD diagnosis that would benefit from medicine because they have a neurological problem. Careful differential diagnosis is needed.

It has only been recently that educators of young children have accepted that there is not a single learning style. Children differ as to how they learn.

This is a good example of the mind-brain synergy. Although well documented, not all school systems have enthusiastically adopted this revised teaching style. Consequently some children experience learning problems and experience the depressive and diminished self-esteem that goes along with poor school performance.

Children can find themselves being teased in school. The schoolyard bully will find something to pick on to tease. The victim will feel awful and feel alone since usually others do not come to his or her rescue lest they become the next target. Some kids who have low self-esteem because of some real or imagined "fault" may worry that it will be noticed and they will be shunned. A noticeable physical disability may attract a bully. The victim will feel scared and angry but need to suppress the feeling. A defensive maneuver "playing the role of clown" may be employed. Here one gets other kids to laugh at your antics or jokes and not at you. It often leads also to disciplinary action as a punishment and then to parental criticism, resulting in reduced secondary narcissism. The whole scenario can lead to much discomfort for the child.

In this section I will include *neurotic* conditions that usually first arise in childhood, can continue into later years, or can appear to go into remission but later reappear. Hence, these dynamic features can manifest across the entire life cycle. I include obsessive-compulsive neurosis, hysteria, hysterical conversion, phobia, and *delinquency*. Earlier, I have referred to neurotic sympto-matology that compromises common life situations, everyday biological functioning, and the expression of inborn talents.

For some children who have disabilities and have suffered as a result, e.g., being teased, they can start to consider themselves as an "exception." They feel they have suffered more than they deserve and they should be exempt in the future from prohibi-tions that others are expected to follow, e.g., sobriety.

Obsessive-compulsive neurosis in the classical sense begins with conflict at the Oedipal phase. As discussed earlier, the child feels threatened and anxious that he will be a victim of physical injury. In a boy's case it is fear of castration at the hands of father in retaliation for his own similar aggression aimed at father in competi-tion with him to usurp his privileges with the boy's mother. In the girl's case the fear is loss of the mother's love because of a similar competition with her to be father's favorite. A regression occurs to an anal fixation. It is in this psychic "arena" that obsessive-compulsive symptoms are formed. The child's Superego is advanced further than a younger child of two or three first dealing with anal impulses and it is intolerant of the child's anal wishes so conflict is felt and compro-mises, symptoms, are sought.

Obsessive thinking involves rumination and concern about details. Compulsive behavior involves repetitive actions without a sense of completion. Together, we have obsessive-compulsive behavior.

The obsessive thought and compulsive actions vary depending on the life experiences of individuals. I will give a couple of ex-amples to illustrate what I mean. A child might be overly concerned about cleanliness, perhaps because of a wish to smear feces, but this is forbidden. However, the unconscious wish although not manifested in action nevertheless causes a sense of guilt and a feeling of physical uncleanliness and a need to wash his or her hands. But washing them once may not be sufficient and it becomes a repetitive action. The child will feel a need, felt as a compulsion to be clean. This child suffers from an obsessive-compulsive neurosis.

Another child may be fearful of an intruder at night. Perhaps this stems from its' own wish to intrude upon his or her parents because of primal scene fantasies in force during the child's Oedipal phase. When such wishes were externalized the child then began to fear a nighttime intruder. With regression to the anal phase, the child again feels unsafe at night because of anal-sadistic wishes that are externalized. The child resorts to locking the door to his room or to the street but is not easily satisfied that he or she is safe. What follows is a repetitive action of unlocking the locked door (s) and relocking them to make sure it is secure. However, the feeling of safety is not satisfied and the action needs to be repeated. This child is involved in an obsessive-compulsive neurosis.

As either of the above children age their obsessive-compulsive neurosis will likely continue although the symptoms may change as the Ego attempts to better defend against conflicted desires. Derivatives of the original wishes will be operative in the now older child as an adolescent, later as an adult, unless therapy or psychoanalysis affords them some emotional understanding and relief via a better solution to the original conflict.

In classical *hysteria* the Oedipal child is conflicted with anxiety because of forbidden sexual desires and aggressive wishes towards parental objects. Girls usually are more prone to this neurotic development than are boys. Perhaps this is because sexual expression in behavior is more culturally acceptable in females than males. A girl may be coquettish and flirtatious, especially with father, in a manner that only a five-year-old girl can express. A boy may be boastful of his strength, especially with mother, also in a manner that only a five-year-old boy can be. The Ego of both children resorts to defensive maneuvers. The forbidden impulses are repressed. Such children may regard themselves and same gendered parent as weak and their opposite gendered parent as powerful, even aggrandized. Present, too, often is an oral fixation underlying the hyper sexuality, suggesting a reservoir of dependency. This may account for the self-image portrayed as weak.

As the child becomes adolescent a "hyper sexuality" or seductiveness becomes a feature of the girl's personality. However, if responded to by a boy the girl becomes scared and retreats. It is as if the seductiveness of the girl is an unconscious maneuver to bring forth potential danger to be avoided in her surroundings. Hence, the boy who is attracted to the girl's coquettishness will be avoided.

As the hysterical adolescent girl becomes adult the features of their adolescent self will continue. They will have consolidated into a hysterical character and the behavior will be labeled histrionic. Intimacy of a sexual kind is avoided. These women may have trouble in relationships with men.

There is a manifestation of hysteria mostly in children and adolescents but sometimes in older patients that we call *hysterical identification*. A child will adopt the physical disability or symptom of a person they are competitive and envious with. For example, a latency age girl who harbors competitive Oedipal level wishes towards mother, may find herself unconsciously identifying with mother's abdominal pains that she believes are due to pregnancy. The girl may complain of abdominal pain that requires medical intervention but no physical cause can be diagnosed. This is because the pain is psychologically induced via identification brought on by envy.

Phobia is another classical neurotic manifestation that can be present in all stages of life and last for a long time. Phobic feelings need to be distinguished from objective fears. If a child has been bitten in the past by a spider, it would be expected they would demonstrate some fear in the presence of a nearby spider. A child with a spider phobia, however, has not been bitten, yet they act terrified in the presence of one. This is because the spider unconsciously represents a different "thing." The spider is like a symbol of something or somebody that evokes fear. A *displacement*, a switch from another anxiety evoking entity, has taken place unconsciously. If what is "chosen" is something usually not in close proximity to the child it will turn out to be a "good" choice. That the child is anxious about being bitten suggests an oral fixation is a determinant. Analyses of children with phobias may illuminate castration fear as a determinant. So in boys, the spider symbolizes the Oedipal rival for mother's love. The famous case of "Little Hans" written up by Freud describes these dynamics. This boy was afraid of being bitten by a horse, a displacement from father, in the streets of Vienna. Later, his difficulties with his mother were illustrated in a later publication, making more sense of his oral expression of castration anxiety.

Other Issues may also trigger a phobia. For example, a *school phobia* may result in a child refusing to go to school. This can last for an extended period of time. Child analysis might clarify that the child is really afraid of leaving home. This may be because of separation issues or anxiety about some harm coming to his or her mother. The imagined harm might be an expression of the child's own anger felt unconsciously towards the mother. Often, such a child will complain of a "stomach ache." Perhaps, the child feels that if he is "ill" the mother will take care of him or her? Hence a displacement from home (mother) to school has taken place.

There are also instances of *counter-phobia* wherein a child may participate or seek out what they are afraid about. For example, if there is a phobia of falling from a high height, the child might engage in tree climbing, without conscious awareness of the underlying dynamic.

CHAPTER 7

Adolescent Psychopathology

In this section I will focus on those conflicts that manifest themselves primarily in adolescence. Two major psychological events that adolescents contend with are increased independence from parents or other custodial adults and the advent of puberty. It is not that efforts at achieving autonomy only begin in the adolescent years but they intensify immeasurerably. The toddler when he or she starts to walk experiences beginning independence and the separation from parents causes them some modicum of *separation anxiety* and they often quickly change their direction back towards the parent for renewed comfort. The two or three year old undergoing toilet mastery will often protest the adults' directions about when and where to defecate. So called "toilet battles" can ensue. The wish for independence continues to grow with school entry but it becomes full blown in adolescence. Peer recognition and acceptance of peer rules, sometimes conflicting with parental rules, becomes a major issue for most adolescents. They want to be socially accepted and popular. Of course, that is not true for all adolescents. Friction with parents can cause family disharmony and stress for all members. In some instances, an adolescent may sense that a parent is holding onto them because of the parent's own insecurity. This could heighten the adolescent's ambivalence about becoming more independent. Intrapsychically, adolescents may feel a loss of the former security provided by an inner sense of bondedness with a strong available parental internalized image. Depressive feelings may arise.

Part of becoming independent is owning one's own body. Prior to adolescence a child accepts that the primary caregiver, usually mother, owns his or her body. They are dependent on mother to take care of his or her body, feed it and nurture it. It is not unusual to see adolescents walking around in the middle of winter in short sleeves, whereas adults around them wear a heavy coat. Owning one's own body can be a stressful situation if the child has an illness like juvenile diabetes. Mother will be protective and reluctant to relinquish control when her child becomes a teenager. The teenager will feel over-controlled and angry.

Use of drugs during adolescence can be detrimental. Recent research suggests that use of marijuana can be harmful to the developing brain of adolescents. Also, daily use of "grass" has been shown to diminish motivation to be active and deal with tasks. The adolescent will experience school achievement and learning difficulties. There can be peer pressure to imbibe that some adolescents cannot refuse for fear of being ostracized. Of course, overuse of stronger drugs can cause death.

Some adolescents will cut themselves, usually on the arm. This action, of course, alarms parents and they seek professional help. Surprisingly, most of the adolescents are not so alarmed. In my experience and that of colleagues the self-cutting is less a sign of self-destruction and, counter-intuitively, more a sign of the adolescent's proclamation of a strength of self—survival.

Puberty begins for many adolescents around age thirteen. Most adolescents welcome it but others are conflicted. Often girls become pubertal earlier than their male counterparts. It is not unusual in a beginning high school class to see girls much taller than the boys. The beginning of menses is welcomed by some girls and abhorred by others. A lot depends on the preparation provided by mothers and/or older sisters. It will be a positive sign of healthy development and future maternity for girls that have been well prepared. Regretfully, for others it could be a messy ordeal they are obliged to take care of. For some girls developing breasts and curvature of their bodies are unwelcomed and they may slouch in posture or wear baggy clothes to hide the changes. Other girls welcome the changes. For the former group sexual desires may cause anxiety, and for the latter exciting fantasies of sexual intimacy.

For boys, puberty may bring on unexpected erections at times that would be embarrassing, e.g., if called upon by a teacher to go up to the front of the classroom to the blackboard. Also, the adolescent boy often greets spontaneous emissions during sleep with displeasure and embarrassment.

Puberty brings forth sexual desires and adolescents must deal with them. Conflicts about sexual expression can be a cause of **much** discomfort during this stage of life. This can be because many adolescents do not distinguish between fantasy and action. They feel, embarrassment, shame, or guilt about both as if they are equivalent. But they are not. In dealing with conflicts about sexual desire many neurotic symptoms can arise. For example, daily masturbation, isolation, anxiety around perceived "sexy" peers, etc.

Precocious puberty can occur in girls during the latency years, usually due to some hormonal disorder. The girls and family are not prepared for it and much discomfort can be experienced. Parents are concerned and worried about the physical and mental health of their daughters. The issues diverge based on the personal psychology of all the participants. Some fathers are uneasy about a physically mature girl sitting on their lap. Some mothers, unsure of their own feminine attractiveness to their husbands, may have to deal with competitive feelings with their daughters for their husbands' interest.

Sexual desire, either heterosexual or homosexual can be a source of discomfort for adolescents. We discussed this earlier when the topic was considered of biological needs getting caught up in conflict. Of course sexual needs are not only biological but also psychological. The topic will be further discussed when we consider adult psychopathology.

When a heterosexual adolescent boy starts to feel sexual desire he notices a girl and may get an erection. Fantasies may preoccupy him and masturbation may follow. For most boys they are uneasy about the need to get up the courage to interact with the girl. Adolescents usually boys and girls together "hang out" in groups. Heterosexual girls are also anxious about dealing with boys. They feel a lot of pressure from boys in these contemporary times to engage in fellatio, a practice they may feel compelled to oblige even though they may prefer not to. For both girls and boys, there is competition with other adolescents regarding attractiveness to the other gender, and jealousy may be intense.

Masturbation, for both genders, is a normal adolescent sexual activity. However, if it becomes a substitute for relating to others, it can be a preoccupation and further inhibit personal interaction.

Younger children, particularly boys can be seen to touch the genital region. Parents best deal with this by not being punitive. They may say to the child that the activity is best done privately in the bedroom. Girls are less obvious in their masturbatory activities, such as squeezing their thighs together or pressing up their groin against a hard surface. Parents that object and insult the child may be fostering sexual anxiety. Unfortunately, this is not so uncommon.

Homosexual adolescents are faced with being "different," "although times are changing." Nevertheless, gay and lesbian adolescents must deal with isolation from the mainstream and shaming, sometimes subtle, from their peers. A support group of like-minded peers is very helpful. For some adolescents being homosexual is likely biological. Recall that during the Oedipal stage the child has sexual feelings for both parents, albeit usually those for the opposite gendered parent being stronger. Many homosexual male adolescents will tell you that they preferred to play with girls and girl's toys from earliest times, and lesbian adolescents may state they always wanted to be playing with boys and their toys as young girls. Many girls, however, labeled as "tomboys" retain their femininity and do not become lesbians.

Some future homosexuals and lesbians likely have a sexual orientation based on biology and not conflict. There are some homosexual and lesbian adolescents, however, that may be afraid of heterosexuality and this may be the underlying cause of their retreat from heterosexuality. Competition with the same gendered parent, or unavailability of the opposite gendered parent may sometimes be determinants. While sorting this out, adolescents go through a very difficult and tense time.

As mentioned earlier, in instances where the Superego was inadequately consolidated or weak, delinquency can be a problem for adolescents. This is especially so if the adolescent gets involved with a peer group where *acting-out* is prevalent. Then the norms of society are compromised. Petty thievery like shoplifting, smoking marijuana, use of drugs like cocaine and opioids, can be a frequent occurrence. Often this results in judiciary involvement and a criminal record that can be a burden for the adolescent in later years in seeking employment. Many young adults regret such past behavior, are ashamed, and will benefit from community support.

An adolescent may associate achieving in school as an acceptance of leaving childhood. They may object because of feeling dependent on adults for their sense of security. Such an adolescent may not expend effort and look as if they have a learning deficiency.

CHAPTER 8

Adult Psychopathology

C haracter styles are formed gradually and are consolidated in the adult years and are not easily abandoned. Character disorders or personality disorders hence are features of adulthood. We saw antecedents in neurotic symptomatology of earlier years. Thus a child who is obsessive and compulsive likely will develop character defenses consistent with such symptoms and as an adult will become an obsessional personality.

Some of the more common *personality* or *character disorders* are *narcissistic, antisocial, obsessive, hysterical, paranoid, dependent, schizoid, depressive,* and *dissociative*. Sometimes a personality type is a mixture of two types. The severity of each is on a continuum from mild to severe. This will depend on life experiences that either mitigated the need for such defenses or stimulated constant use of them to build a protective shield.

A *narcissistic personality* is someone who underneath the bravado feels very insecure. To distance themselves from low self-esteem they focus on "me" and brag about their accomplishments. They come across as knowing everything because they are "omniscient." Everything that they do is described as the "best" and they are always listening for compliments and crave applause. As children they may have been schoolyard "bullies," in a futile attempt to bolster low self-esteem. Some narcissists may have had in their youth an idealized grandparent as a model that a parent had for them to live up to. Failure to succeed in this goal, the future narcissist may compensate by acting as if they know everything and are the best at everything.

An *anti-social personality* believes in an individual moral code that benefits only him or her. The Superego of such individuals is weak or corrupt. Selfish gain to strengthen one's power over others is of paramount importance, not behavior that is aware of other's well being. As adolescents such individuals were delinquent. In instances where this personality is pervasive, criminal behavior and incarceration may occur. Often such individuals have identified with anti-social parents or peers that are delinquent.

Obsessive personality types are rigid and governed by private thoughts. They cannot relax and feel free of anxiety until they have achieved a goal. Failure to do so results in a sense of failure. Compulsive acts are in the interest of achieving "perfection." This is not accepted as an unattainable ideal that can only be approximated. Not being "perfect" leaves them very insecure. Sometimes the compulsive acts are to avoid an anxiety producing activity or fantasy, e.g., cleaning house to avoid sexual excitement.

An individual with a *hysterical personality* usually comes across as histrionic, given to dramatic story telling, with lots of emotional accompaniments. Exaggeration is the standard, covering over a sense of thinking oneself as boring and trivial. Such a woman may be flirtatious in a defensive manner insofar as this covers over a fear of sexuality and intimacy.

A *paranoid personality* believes other people cannot be trusted. They are conspiring to take advantage of you because of envy. Such suspiciousness covers over a sense of personal inadequacy. Relationships are few because they require intimacy and letting down your guard. Having fun is a rarity.

A *dependent personality* relies on the protection of another person that is viewed as strong and capable of looking after your wellbeing as well as his or her own. In some respects they are parental surrogates to make up for deficiencies of one's own. Such dependency requires that others act towards you as if they think you are worthwhile to compensate for a lack of self-esteem. In a marriage, tension and bickering can be frequent if a spouse is very dependent insofar as it is unreasonable to expect a spouse to be a parent too.

People who were loners by choice used to be thought of as having a *schizoid personality*. This term is rarely used today. It described individuals who avoided relationships likely because of latent hostility towards primary figures in the past who were disappointments. Such avoidance made it less likely that hostile aggressive behavior would come to the surface. Solitary activities are sought and occupational choices made where interaction or group participation can be avoided. A good example would be to work alone in a laboratory.

A *depressive personality* often feels rejected by others and blames him or her self because of personal inadequacies. They may always feel "empty," and lonely. Such negative feelings about the self are derivatives from earlier life experiences in childhood and/or adolescence.

"Dissociative" may be a word that you are not familiar with. Someone with a *dissociative personality* unconsciously seems to characteristically change his or her self-identity. It is as if they temporarily forget who they are. Such individuals often have been abused in the past and this defensive wall is an existential attempt to survive.

In a consultation it is not infrequent that adults will in their account of their past speak of an over-bearing, authoritative father. This is particularly difficult for males. It is as if they never felt that they pleased their fathers. Or it might be remembered that they thought a parent was not very warm so that they rarely felt cared for. With treatment this narrative might be revised for some of them. They might recognize that their memories were exaggerated and that their grandparents were not model parents either. The latter would allow some forgiveness for their parents' shortcomings. Unfortunately, in many instances the sense of having experienced unsatisfying parenting remained. Or they identified with the parenting they experienced and repeated it with their own children.

In addition to psychological conflicts that began in childhood or adolescence and are continued into later life or re-experienced later in a derivative form, there are issues that are specific to adulthood. These events are experienced by all of us and in most instances we cope adaptively with them and the solutions are favorable. When they are not we can feel anxious and/or depressed or other unfavorable feelings. Sometimes dealing with these issues re-kindles earlier mental conflicts that may have become latent. I am thinking of issues, in the usual chronological order in which they appear, such as applying to college, leaving the parental home, choosing a future occupation or career, and becoming comfortable with a sexual orientation. With increasing age, one deals with issues such as choosing a life partner, deciding on becoming a parent, dealing with an "empty nest," dealing with aging parents as one's self is getting older. Then, dealing with retirement, old age, health changes, and finally coming to terms with existential anxiety.

The above issues are *psychosocial,* as well as psychodynamic. That is, in addition to individual and familial psychodynamics, there are societal expectations, rewards or obstacles that can either facilitate or hinder the successful achieving of these goals. Let us imagine, a late adolescent African-American girl from the rural South who aspires to be an astrophysicist. Her parents have always told her that they believed "she could be whatever she wants to be." So, possessing a high degree of Ego strength and motivation she is an honor student in high school and is given a scholarship to a renowned university. The people in her new sur-roundings all like her because of her winning personality but may harbor private doubts about the likelihood she will be successful. They have preconceived ideas about a female Black student who grew up on a farm getting a Ph.D. in astrophysics. Outside of the academic community such doubts will exist. The doubts are pre-conceived biases. This is an extreme example of negative psychosocial dynamics at play that can interact with personal conflict-laden psychodynamics. Such obstacles need to be overcome by young adults, particularly young women, making life choices. You can expect that there will be a high degree of stress for most of these young adults.

Choice of career used to be decided to a great degree by what your father had chosen. It would be "Father & Son." In contemporary times this expectation is considerably reduced, although in some families it may remain and when not met feelings of disloyalty may exist, albeit under the surface. Nowadays, there are numerous choices for young adults. Women, too, have opportunities that were never normal expectations in years past. Advances in technology have created occupations that did not exist in an earlier generation. Acquiring a skill in a trade has lost its appeal in contemporary society. Hence, choosing a career can cause lots of doubts and insecurities.

Training for a career choice may mean separating from the parental home. If a college education is part of the preparation, it may mean moving a distance from parents. Having practiced in a college town for years, I am familiar with the frequent manifestation of separation anxiety, depressive feelings, and loneliness reported by college students. Suicidal thoughts also can occur. When these feelings are intense and result in poor school performance and a sense of isolation, the young adult may take a leave of absence, or hopefully, seek professional help. Presumably such intense reactions have their antecedents in childhood or during adolescence when the relationship with parents was fraught with difficulties. The possible causes are too numerous to list, but I am thinking of such family dynamics as parental divorce, an alcoholic parent, abuse by a parent, etc.

Becoming comfortable with a sexual orientation is not easy for some young adults. Many may feel comfortable to the gender they are attracted to but unable to act upon their desire. They feel a *sexual inhibition.* The cause most likely has an earlier origin having to do with self-condemnation for what they thought were illicit choices that would evoke guilt or external punishment from perceived rivals. I am thinking of unresolved positive Oedipal desires.

The binary classification of heterosexual and homosexual has proven to be not inclusive enough. We discussed this earlier in the section on adolescent psychopathology. Some young adults feel bisexual. In our observations of young children and our theory of the Oedipal complex this is thought to be universal, albeit one parent is more "sexually" desirable than the other for most children. In adolescence one inclination usually becomes much stronger than the other. For most boys, they are sexually attracted to girls, for most girls they are sexually attracted to boys. Some children seem to always have been attracted to their own gender, and here it can be attributed to a biological determinant. However, for some children such an early attraction likely was due to conflict and defensive.

It is only recently that homosexuality has been a "accepted," although on a latent level for many it is not, particularly among religiously observant people.

Gay men and lesbian women often feel ostracized and condemned from the larger community. They feel hurt and angry. A few feel guilty, stemming from early internalized moral beliefs, or because of feeling they have disappointed their parents. Some parents mourn the future absence of grandchildren, although with adoption as an option and surrogate conception this can be overcome.

Sexual perversions or *paraphilias* are sexual disturbances that some adults, usually males, experience. For these individuals sexual intercourse is not sufficiently satisfying, and maybe an experience that deprives them of an orgasm. Foreplay, in "healthy" sex is meant to arouse the participants so that coitus can occur and orgasm can be reached.

However, adults with perversions do not achieve this outcome. The feeling states vary among perverts. Some are privately and secretly planning an encounter in fantasy and/or actuality wherein the perversion can be satisfied. Sometimes a partner will comply begrudgingly in order "to keep the peace." After the experience the pervert may feel a heightened good feeling like elation, but soon there- after they may feel alone and depressed.

There are many different perversions. Exhibitionism, such as exposing one's genitals to a stranger or to a child may be acted upon. Voyeurism, such as being a "peeping Tom" looking with binoculars through the window of an adjacent neighbor's house to view an adolescent girl's nudity as she undresses. Fetishism is the required presence of a thing, usually an item of clothing such as a woman's shoe, during sexual intimacy to get full pleasure. Or it can be required focus on a specific body part such as a foot of the sexual partner. Pedophilia, or a sexual desire of children, is often the motive for sexual abuse of children. Transvestism, dressing up as the other gender during sex may be required. Sexual masochism and sadism are two common perversions. It may mean requiring bondage of oneself or one's partner to enjoy sexual intercourse, or it could involve inflicting some pain on one's partner or having it inflicted on oneself in order to get sexual pleasure.

Acceptance of one's birth gender is not a simple matter for some young adults, or as adolescents earlier. *Transgender* issues are more and more in our awareness. Such adolescents and young adults feel isolated from other youth or young adults. They can become intensely depressed and suicidal. Their parents are confused. They do not know how to respond. They want to be supportive but they may believe the child is behaving dramatically or irrationally. They feel that the child is confused and with therapy they will change his or her mind. Young adults and older adults who elect to obtain first hormonal treatment and then surgical interventions aimed at transforming their gender are more frequent in this decade alone than earlier ones. Some will elect only to be *transvestites* and dress in the clothes of the other preferred gender.

Undoubtedly, some young people who are unaccepting of their gender are feeling so because of conflict, for example, not wanting to "turn out" to be like an abusive parent, but others feel intensely that their self-identity does not correspond to the body they possess.

Choosing a life partner has been delayed in the current generation compared to mine. People nowadays do not choose to commit themselves to another until sometimes into there thirties. Also, some elect to live together but not to marry. Perhaps this is due to the decline of religious values. In any case, choosing a partner to commit to can be a source of psychological distress for some. Are they in a love that feels to be enduring? They are aware of divorce if they marry but would rather not have to go through such an event. Or is the choice made out of convenience? Two people like each other, have similar interests, sex is good, so why not live together? The choice of a partner sometimes may have unconscious undertones. What I am thinking of, is choosing someone who is like a parent, perhaps because of pre-Oedipal unmet or indulged dependency issues, or because of Oedipal issues having to do with frustrated childhood sexual desires and competitive wishes with a parental rival. It is during adolescence that the choice of a person to be connected to can be a resolved outcome of successfully severed ties to Oedipal and pre-Oedipal objects. If this has not been accomplished the marriage or partnership may be fraught with disappointment. After all, the adult partner you have chosen is not your parent and childhood wishes will not be satisfied to the level required by your unconscious desire. The outcome likely will be marital tension, fighting, and possibly divorce.

Choosing to become a parent can be met with joyful expectations. If infertility is an unexpected outcome, depressive feelings will become obvious.

Adoption, artificial insemination, and conceptual surrogacy are contemporary solutions. Nevertheless, the infertile partner may still feel inadequate and self-esteem may suffer. Infidelities in the marriage can be a reaction to the disappointment.

Becoming a parent in most instances has an emotional connection to the parenting that you experienced as a child. Will you be a better parent than your own or be unable to "live up" to the good example they put forth? If you had a "bad" parent likely you swore to be different. Unfortunately, the psychic mechanism of identification may be stronger than your vow. As a way of mastering your disappointment you may turn a passive experi-ence into an active one and unwittingly do to your child what you endured. Here the phenomenon of intergenerational trans-mission of pathology is given expression.

Having children enter the family can be difficult for some men. Women seem to be more instinctively parental while men are becoming more so as our culture accepts such behavior. It is no longer believed to be un-masculine to change a diaper, sooth an infant, etc, than it once was. However, regretfully, there still will be some men who will feel displaced by their wife's attention to a child. Marital tension can result. In extreme cases, divorce can be an outcome.

For many parents, the success of their children in life brings them great pleasure. For some, they feel responsible to a greater degree than they objectively are and rob the child of its accom-plishments. They own the success and they talk to their friends as if that is so. The child can become aware of this and feel anger. Some parents go the other path; they take an inordinate sense of responsibility for their child's failures in life. They are totally to blame for their bad parenting. You can see that good parenting is an asset for a child. The child, too, independently is a large factor in future success or failure.

Dealing with a so-called "empty nest" can be difficult for some parents. It is less so for those parents who have had additional interests to parenting, e.g., a career or talent that they let develop. Regretfully, for some it can lead to feelings of abandonment and depression, likely stimulated by earlier childhood losses. For some parents, mostly men, it can result in extramarital affairs as a way of reinforcing their sense of manhood diminished by no longer being a provider to a family. Others may deal with the loss by purchasing something of value that they unconsciously wish will enhance their image as a worthwhile adult, like a new expensive auto.

Retirement is something that is delayed more so now than in earlier generations. This is especially so among adults who have professional careers where physical aging has less of an impact, unless, of course, if there is a decline in cognitive functioning. When one retires, there may be diminished self-esteem insofar as one's occupation or career likely afforded the adult a feeling of competence and accomplishment as well as recognition of such from others. For some older adults, this loss of self-esteem can be intense and lead to depression. The same issues as in the "empty nest" experience are involved. Are there other interests that can be enjoyed? Can one be more involved with one's spouse?

Becoming a grandparent can be a source of great pleasure and a feeling of accomplishment for most older adults. There exists a sense of pride in the accomplishment of one's children becoming parents. When grandchildren do not exist older adults can feel envy of friends who are grandparents.

A grandparent must recognize they are not parents to their grandchildren. They can, however, impart the wisdom of their years and support the healthy parenting of their own children, and in some instances diminish the bad outcome of poor parenting by their own children. For some grandparents whose children are unable to be parents to their own children, perhaps because of drug addiction or incarceration, they are asked to become guardians of their grandchildren. This can be burdensome for those who are not physically capable or impoverished but most, nevertheless, do a needed job that benefits the grandchildren.

Older age is a time when one's own parents get ill or die. As parents' age and need the assistance of their grown up children, most children agreeably do so. They feel grateful for the care and devotion given them and they wish to reciprocate. However, for some it is felt burdensome, presumably because of a perceived history of neglect. Such older adults will be latently angry and some will feel guilty because of this.

Mourning is an experience we all endure as we age. Not only parents but also friends, who are contemporaries, die. With old age, however, we must come to terms with our own eventual death. We call this *existential anxiety*. Older adults differ as to whether or not this is a cause of anxiety. Those who are religiously observant are less bothered because they believe in "life after death," either spiritually or maybe in reincarnation. Most people who are pleased more-or-less with their life attainments are accepting of inevitable death and not anxious or preoccupied about it. They are reassured that they will be well thought of because of the legacy they have left behind. Such individuals feel they have lived a life of integrity that will be honored.

Postscript

Contemporary psychiatry is very much a discipline that views mental disturbances as diseases that can be treated with medication. Sometimes the combined use of drugs and talk therapy is recommended. The intervention of "talk therapy" is often seen in those instances as causing a change, along with the administration of drugs, in the brain effecting an alleviation of symptoms. The mind is almost never conceptualized as the site of mental conflict causing distressing feelings like anxiety, shame, or guilt resulting in compromise formations, or symptoms. It is as if "mental illness" is thought to be akin to Alzheimer's disease where plaque and tangles invade synapses leaving cognitive and mental deficiencies in their path. Another example is the brains of patients suffering from post-concussion, demonstrating cognitive and affect regulation problems. I expect that a modern day psychiatrist would accuse me of being extreme in my criticism. The mind and the brain are connected. Let us not forget that Freud started out as a neurologist but he saw the value in investigating the mind. Someday in the distant future the connections between the two will be illuminated, but I believe alleviating mental anguish will still come from emotionally understanding of mental conflicts and not from taking a pill. Plato and Socrates once said that a life not understood is a life not worth living.

In contemporary psychiatry, psychoanalysis is usually thought of as a discredited pseudo-science. The uninformed public, for the most part, has accepted this viewpoint. Or the public wants a "quick fix." If therapy is going to fix the problem it must remove the symptoms. Hence behavior modification therapy or its cousins are sought after, no matter the cause of the symptoms. Medical insurance rarely covers psychoanalysis and the fees charged can be afforded by only a few. This needs to be re-considered. Low fee clinics desperately need to be established.

Earlier, I stressed my opinion, and that of many psychoanalytic colleagues, that childhood development and problems experienced by the child during these early years lay the foundation for future psychopathology. Anna Freud, whose writings were groundbreaking, is rarely referred to in contemporary literature on development and psychopathology. The logic of this defies me. Her insights are invaluable.

All of the above distresses me and was one of my motives for writing this book. I wished to show the dynamic complexities of mental conflict, its effect on people, and the attempts to resolve them, often resulting in neurosis. I also want to show that mental "illness" can be understood, that it is not a conundrum of unexplainable thoughts and feelings that best be avoided. My hope is that I have come at least within sight of this objective.

Representative List of Topics

PREFACE
Overview of book; Style of book

ESSENTIAL CONCEPTS IN UNDERSTANDING PSYCHOPATHOLOGY
Sexual & Aggressive Drive; phases; gratification; complemental series; fixation; regression; foundation for later psychopathology; intergenerational transmission of psychopathology; mental conflict; anxiety; in trapsychic, internalized, external conflicts; passive/active aims; sublimation; psychological mindedness; sadism/masochism; trauma; narcissism; self-esteem.

LIFE EVENTS AND PSYCHOPATHOLOGY
Death of a loved one or pet; inability to mourn; suicide; survivor guilt; Genocide; adoption; infertility; Divorce; sexual abuse; emotional abuse; Internet pornography; identification with the abuser; sibling rivalry; racial and religious bigotry.

BASIC BIOLOGICAL FUNCTIONS THAT MAY DRAWN INTO CONFLICT
Sleep; eating; breast-feeding; toileting; Urination; locomotion; sexual expression; Bisexuality; gender.

NATURAL STRENGTHS INTERFERED WITH BY PSYCHOPATHOLOGY
Curiosity; Athleticism; Musical ability.

DIAGNOSTIC CATEGORIES
Borderline; Depression; Neurosis; Character; Developmental interferences; Developmental Conflicts (e.g.Oedipus Complex); Psychosomatic; Hypochondria.

Childhood Psychopathology

Preoedipal; attachment disorders; Temper tantrums; procrastination; learning disabilities; passive-aggressive; reaction formation behavior; conduct disorder; oppositional-defiant disorder; attention deficit-hyperactivity disorder; teasing; childhood neurosis; obsessive- compulsive neurosis; hysteria; hysterical Identification; phobia; school phobia; counter-phobia.

Adolescent Psychopathology

Independence strivings; Self-cutting; Puberty; precocious puberty in girls; Sexual desire; heterosexuality; masturbation; Homosexuality; acting out; marijuana use.

Adult Psychopathology

Narcissistic personality; Anti-social personality; Obsessive personality; Hysterical personality; Paranoid Personality; Dependent personality; Schizoid personality; Depressive pe rsonality; Dissociative personality; Occupational or career choice; Sexual orientation; Binary gender classification; Homosexuality;
Sexual perversion; Transgender issues; Choosing a life partner; Parenthood; "Empty nest"; Retirement; Grand parenthood; Illness, mourning; existential; anxiety.

Postscript

Goal in writing book.

Recommended Readings

CHILDHOOD PSYCHOPATHOLOGY

(Annuals and complete works.)
Psychoanalytic Study of the Child (PSC),
Volumes 1-25, International Universities Press
Volumes 26- 27, Quadrangle Press
Volumes 28-65, Yale University Press
Volumes 70-71, Routledge Press
Child Analysis, Hanna-Perkins Center for Child Development, Volumes 1-18
Bulletin of the Hampstead Clinic, 1978-1984; renamed Bulletin of the Anna Freud Centre, 1985-1995
Journal of the American Psychoanalytic Association (JAPA) Search www.pep-web.org for appropriate articles.
The Writings of Anna Freud, International Universities Press (IUP) Volumes 1-8, 1936-1980.

(Selected articles and books.)
Corbett, K. 2009, Boyhoods: rethinking Masculinities. New Haven, Yale University Press
Decarie, Gouin, T. 1974, The Infants Reaction to Strangers, IUP, Madison, CT.
Erikson, E. 1963, Childhood and Society, Norton, N.Y.
Furman, Erna, 1987 Helping Young Children Grow, IUP, Madison, CT
1993, Toddlers and Their Mothers, IUP, Madison, CT.
1995, Preschoolers: Questions and Answers, IUP, Madison, CT.
2001, On Being and Having a Mother, IUP, Madison, CT.
Fraiberg, Selma, 1959, The Magic Years, Scribner's, N.Y.

Fraiberg, S., Adelson, E., & Shapiro, V., 1975, Ghosts in the Nursery, A psychoanalytic Approach to the problems of impaired infant-mother relationships.

J.Am.Academy of Child & Adolescent Psychiatry, 14, 387-421

Greenspan, S.I. & Pollock, G.H. (Eds.), 1981, The Course of Life, Vols 1 & 2, NIMH.

Lax, R.F., Bach,S., & Burland, J.A. (EDs.), 1980, Rapprochement, Jason Aronson, N.Y.

Legg, C., & Sherick, I.,1976, The Replacement Child: A developmental tragedy: Some preliminary comments. Child Psychiatry and Human Development, 7.

Mahler, M.S., Pine, F., & Bergman, A., 1997, The Psychological Birth of the Human Infant, Basic Books, N.Y.

McDevitt, J.B., & Settlage, C., (Eds.) 1971, IUP, Madison, Ct.

Novick, K. & Novick, J., 2019, Emotional Muscle, Xliberis.

Olesker, W. 2011, The Story of Sam. Continuities and Discontinuities in Development, PSC, 65, 48-47.

Parens, H., & Saul, I.J., Dependence: A Psychoanalytic Study, IUP, Madison, CT.

Sherick, I., 1981, The Significance of Pets for Children: Illustrated by a latency Age Girl's Use of Pets in Her Analysis., PSC, 36, 193-215.

——1983, Adoption and Disturbed Narcissism: Case Illustration of a Latency Boy. J.Am.Psa.A., 31, 487-513.

Spitz, R.A., 1965, The First Year of Life, IUP, Madison, CT.

Winnicott, D.W., 1965, The Maturational Processes and the facilitating Environment: Studies in the Theory of Emotional Development. London, Karnac, 1990.

ADOLESCENT PSYCHOPATHOLOGY

Barrett, T.F., 2008, Manic defenses against loneliness in adolescence, PSC, 63, 111-136.

Blos, P. 1962, On Adolescence, Free Press, N.Y.

——1970, Young Adolescence, Free Press, N.Y.

——1979, The Adolescent Passage: Developmental Issues, IUP, Madison, CT.

Brockman, D. D. (Ed.) 1984, Late Adolescence: Psychoanalytic Studies. London, Karnac.

Browning, D.L., 2011, Testing Reality During Adolescence: The Contribution of Erikson's Concepts of Fidelity and Developmental Actuality, Psa.Q., LXXX, 555-594.

Erikson, E., 1963, Childhood & Society, Norton, N.Y.

Deutsch, H., 1967, Selected Problems of Adolescence, Monograph Series of the PSC, Vol.3, IUP, Madison, CT.

Greenspan, S.I., & Pollock, G.H. (Eds.), 1981, The Course of Life, Vol. 2, NIMH.

Katan, A., 1951, The role of displacement in "agoraphobia." Int. J. Psa., 32, 41- 50.

Marcus, I.M. (Ed.), 1975, Masturbation, IUP, Madison, CT.

ADULT PSYCHOPATHOLOGY

Colarusso, C. 1992, Child & Adult Development, Plenum, N.Y.

Erikson, E., 1963, Childhood & Society, Norton, N.Y.

Freud, S.1886-1939, The Complete Psychological Works of Sigmund Freud, Vols 1- 23, Standard Edition, Hogarth, London.

Greenspan, S.I., & Pollock, G.H. (Eds.) The Course of Life, Vol. 3, NIMH

ADDITIONAL REFERENCE

PSYCHODYNAMIC DIAGNOSTIC MANUAL (PDM) 2006, Silver Springs, MD. {Collaborative effort: Am Psa Assn, Int Psa Assn, APA (Div 39), Am Academy of Psa and Dynamic Psychiatry, & Psa in Clinical SW.}

www.ingramcontent.com/pod-product-compliance
Lightning Source LLC
Chambersburg PA
CBHW071247020426
42333CB00015B/1663